INSPIRATIONAL BASKETBALL STORIES FOR YOUNG READERS

12 UNBELIEVABLE TRUE TALES TO INSPIRE AND AMAZE YOUNG BASKETBALL LOVERS

Mike Johnson

ISBN: 979-8-89095-004-8

CONTENTS

ATTENTION:

DO YOU WANT MY FUTURE BOOKS AT HEAVY DISCOUNTS AND EVEN FOR FREE?

HEAD OVER TO WWW.SECRETREADS.COM **AND JOIN MY SECRET BOOK CLUB!**

INTRODUCTION

Among all of the major professional sports around the world, basketball is one of the most accessible and creative. From a young age, players learn how to manipulate the ball, and their opponents, in an effort to accomplish their goals. And, thankfully, a young player only needs to bring one ball to the local park. Because of this accessibility, college and professional basketball is full of individuals who have worked their way up from difficult times, making a life of dreams for themselves and those around them.

Even those who did not struggle in their early years often understand the camaraderie that comes from being on a basketball team. It's not like a football squad of 50 or more players. Instead, 12 players share a bench, and only five can play at a time, but the team works hard to improve and win.

This book will look at 12 inspiring stories from the world of basketball, all of which are driven by talented individuals who demonstrate how the game can be beautiful, masterful, tricky, and devastating. In these pages, you'll experience how the flu almost altered NBA history forever. You'll see a father support his daughter in her time of need, and then return to his team when they needed him the most. This book will also show you how one of the game's biggest players is also making a massive impact on the world after his retirement.

Inspirational Basketball Stories has these moments and more, all waiting for you to explore and learn more about the game you already love.

One thing to remember as you're reading these stories is that the game of basketball is truly one that can be played by anyone. If you are a young person who loves the game, you have the opportunity to develop that skill and use it to propel your life forward. If you have passed that time in your life, you still have the chance to guide a young player forward.

All it takes is dedication and a passion for the game. If you don't have those just yet, maybe the stories in this book will help to motivate you.

Get ready for the tipoff!

CHAPTER 1:

2006 GEORGE MASON PATRIOTS

In the sport of basketball, there is one tournament that captures the attention of fans all around the country and even the world. Sure, the NBA Playoffs and the Olympics are great events, but there is only one event that gives dozens of teams an opportunity for glory.

Sixty-eight teams from around the country compete for the championship, and every team represents a different college or university in the United States. The NCAA Men's Basketball Tournament that happens every year in March, also known as March Madness, is that tournament, and by its very nature, it provides great stories of inspiration.

Every once in a great while, a lesser-known team claws its way through their stronger, wealthier opponents and catches the imagination of those watching at home. This chapter is the story of one of those teams, the 2006 George Mason Patriots.

If you've never heard of this basketball team before, don't worry, you're not alone. The George Mason Patriots, representing George Mason University, play in a conference called the Colonial Athletic Association. This small conference consists of teams mostly collected along the eastern coast of the United States, and it features schools such as Old Dominion, Hofstra, Virginia Commonwealth University, and Georgia State.

These are not the biggest or best schools when it comes to athletic competition, especially basketball. If you're looking for the big names, the teams that make it far into the tournament year after year, you're better off looking at the schools like Duke, North Carolina, Kentucky, Virginia, and Kansas. Those are the big schools with lots of scholarship money to attract the best talent.

But anything can happen when the game starts. In the NCAA Men's Basketball Tournament, a school doesn't need to win a best-of-seven series to advance to the next round. Instead, each round is a single game. If you lose one game in the tournament, your season is over. Anything can happen in one game.

During the 2005–2006 regular season, the Patriots had a pretty good year, by their standards. They set a school record with 23 wins in the regular season, and they even briefly made it into the Top 25 rankings for teams around the country.

However, before even reaching the big tournament, the Patriots suffered two substantial losses, both at the hands of a conference opponent, Hofstra. Because of these losses, they fell out of the Top 25 and did not win their conference tournament. They also lost games to bigger schools during the season, teams such as Wake Forest and Creighton, but these were not unexpected. Those losses to Hofstra, though, did not bode well for their momentum moving forward. Some experts even argued that George Mason was not playing well enough to be selected for the NCAA Tournament.

Still, they were selected as an 11th seed to play in the big tournament, marking the first time they were selected without being a conference champion. But because of that low seed, they had to face a strong opponent in the first round. It was none other than the Michigan State Spartans, a team that had made it all the way to the Final Four in the previous year's tournament.

Michigan State was a team that was known for its strong defense, but so was George Mason. Between the two, one of them had to give. It would come down to which team would perform better in the portion of the court called "the lane" or "the paint." That's the portion of the court directly in front of, and under, the basket. Teams who are strong and physical with their play often like to play here. Good defensive teams love to play in these games.

At the end of this first-round match, it was the George Mason Patriots who found themselves advancing to the next round, fueled by Folarin Campbell and his 21 points. The final score was 75-65. It was not a blowout, but it was a convincing piece of evidence that this Patriots team did deserve a spot in the tournament. With the critics silenced, only one question remained: How far could they go?

The prevailing expectation was the Patriots' run would end quite soon, as their next opponent was none other than the defending tournament champion, North Carolina. The Patriots' coach, Jim Larranaga, told his players that even though they were facing a superpower team, they just needed to remember that their green jerseys were the same color as kryptonite and that they could slay any superpower. The players were ready for the challenge.

But their opponent came ready to play, too. Very quickly into the game, the North Carolina Tar Heels raced out to a huge 14-point lead.

The George Mason Patriots didn't panic, though. After the first half, they were losing 27-20. That might not seem like a great situation, but they had already removed half of North Carolina's lead, and there was still plenty of game left to play.

Through the second half, the Patriots began heating up, and their great shooting and always-tough defense helped secure an amazing comeback victory, 65-60.

Sometimes, in these tournaments, teams get lucky in their seeding, and they end up playing a couple of teams that might not be the strongest of opponents. A Cinderella team might make it to the Sweet 16 before facing a strong test, and no one thinks twice when that team loses to a powerhouse school. George Mason had played two games in this tournament, and they had slayed two giant schools.

It would only be fair, then, that they would get an opponent with which they were much more familiar. Cue the Wichita State Shockers, a team that has been a frequent visitor to the tournament. However, George Mason had already faced this team in the regular season, a victory for the Patriots. Now, a good team would understand that a victory earlier in the season means nothing in the NCAA tournament. Could George Mason avoid losing to this team?

Thankfully, the team found a way, once again defying the odds and continuing to push further into the tournament. But when a team has won three games in the tournament, it means that there are only eight teams left. This portion of the tourney is called the Elite Eight for a reason, and George Mason was matched up against a very elite opponent. In fact, their opponent was a team that, after a dominant season, many expected to win the tournament. That team was the Connecticut Huskies.

This UConn team was particularly talented, as four of their players would go on to be drafted in the first round of the

NBA draft later that same year. With such a stacked roster, there was little doubt from analysts that George Mason's run would come to an end.

Throughout the game, the analysts seemed to be proven correct. Late in the first half, the Patriots trailed by as many as 12 points. Early into the second half, they trailed by nine. But, thanks to some strong three-point shooting, hitting six in a row as a team, they clawed back into the game and even took the lead late in the match.

They were up four points with 10 seconds left when UConn scored twice, tying the game at the buzzer. This historic matchup was headed to overtime!

In the overtime session, the Patriots continued their strong shooting from the three-point arc, going five for six. They also managed to keep up their strong defenses as the seconds counted down. With an 86-81 lead, the Patriots did everything they could to keep the Huskies from scoring, but a big three-point shot from UConn made the score 86-84 with less than 10 seconds left.

At the free throw line, the Patriots missed, giving UConn the last shot of the game. The Huskies stormed down the floor as the Patriots scrambled to protect their small lead. Just as the last couple of seconds were counting down, UConn took a three-point shot to win the game.

The ball hung in the air for a couple of moments as it headed for the net. The George Mason Patriots watched it fly, their season hanging in the balance. How far they had come when no one had expected them to, and they fought UConn to the very end, even holding leads toward the end of regulation and overtime.

This time, though, there would be no tie when the clock ran out.

The ball descended toward the basket, and clanged off the rim, bouncing away, leaving George Mason victorious over the Connecticut Huskies, shocking the world.

For the first time in 27 years, an 11th-seeded team had made it through the gauntlet to reach the Final Four. Out of the 64 teams that began the tournament that year, there were only four left, and the George Mason Patriots were one of them.

Excitement for the Cinderella story was contagious, but it was strongest at the college itself, which held an impromptu pep rally for their team.

The simple truth is that the team was finding ways to win, and a strong defense was helping them keep their opponents' shooting percentages down. It was a simple plan, but it was working wonders for this team.

A trip to the Final Four is where this story meets its end, though, as the Patriots would lose their next matchup to the eventual tournament champions, the Florida Gators, another powerhouse school with a strong basketball program.

While this story is not a perfect Cinderella story with the amazing ending that everyone sees in the movies, it is still an inspirational story that many can learn from.

There may be times in your life when you are at a disadvantage against other competitors. Maybe you are competing against classmates for the top position in the school band, and you know that some of those other kids have better equipment or more time to practice. Maybe you're applying for a summer job and can't get an interview because all of the privileged kids are getting those jobs.

There are lots of ways in which you can be disadvantaged. However, because of stories like the George Mason Patriots, you can keep in the back of your mind that hard work, dedication, and putting your heart into every ounce of effort is still a combination that can produce results.

You might not always win. That's life, sometimes. However, you can still demonstrate to those around you that your position in the world doesn't mean you're not capable of great things. The 2006 George Mason Patriots showed the world exactly that.

CHAPTER 2:

MICHAEL JORDAN

You can't talk about basketball, dedication, and hard work without mentioning the player most lauded as the greatest to ever walk the court. Most basketball fans around the world have heard of Michael Jordan, if not from his basketball prowess and success, then perhaps by the shoes that bear his name and nickname, 'Air Jordan'.

It's important, though, to take a deeper look and remember not just what Michael accomplished, but how he got there, and how success does not come easy to anyone. After all, the headline of any story will tell you how many championships he won, but the story might not tell you how much work it required.

Michael Jordan was born in New York, but he grew up in North Carolina. As a young high school athlete, Michael played basketball, baseball, and football. Famously, his first setback as a basketball player came during his sophomore year in high school, when he failed to make the varsity basketball team. When he was cut from that tryout, the coach told him that he was too short to excel in the sport.

Imagine someone telling you that you cannot be successful at something you love because of a reason you cannot control. It's a different story when someone tells you that you are lacking the skill or knowledge required for success. Those are things you can go home and improve with practice and study. But when someone tells you that you are genetically unfit for the task, it leaves you powerless, defeated.

Thankfully for Michael Jordan, that would change. During that sophomore year of high school, Jordan played JV basketball and scored a ton of points. Then, that summer, he grew four inches. With his new height and skill display, he played varsity basketball for the remaining two years and earned a scholarship to play at North Carolina.

He did not waste time making an impact at the college level. He was named the Atlantic Coast Conference Freshman of the Year by averaging over 13 points per game on 53% shooting. To cap off the season, he scored the game-winning shot in the NCAA Championship game. Some players make big shots at the high school or college level, and then they're never heard about again. Michael Jordan used the confidence he gained from this shot to propel himself forward.

Over the next two years with North Carolina, he was named a First Team All-American in the NCAA, and then he decided to skip his senior year to enter the 1984 NBA Draft.

You might think that a player with such a rich history in the NBA would have been selected first overall, but this is not the case. After the Houston Rockets selected Hakeem Olajuwon and the Portland Trail Blazers picked Sam Bowie, the Chicago Bulls chose Michael Jordan with the third overall pick. It's easy to wonder what might have happened differently if Jordan had gone to either of those teams.

Regardless, Jordan scored 16 points in his debut game before going on to average over 28 points per game on 51% shooting. Other players around the league, though, were not happy with how popular Jordan was becoming. When Michael was voted into the NBA All-Star Game during his rookie season, a group of other All-Star players tried to take away some of Jordan's momentum. During that All-Star game, some of the players on Jordan's team simply refused to pass the ball to him. They likely hoped that poor performance from him would cause some fans to turn away.

Of course, that was all in vain. But imagine having so much success that you make enemies of your colleagues. It must have been difficult for Jordan to shoulder that burden as he continued his push toward greatness. Remember that others will often be jealous of your success, so be sure to protect yourself as you continue to move forward with your goals and dreams.

At the end of his rookie season, the Bulls lost to the Milwaukee Bucks in the first round of the playoffs. Jordan was named Rookie of the Year, but he was not even close to satisfied. With his help, though, the Chicago Bulls were suddenly much closer to being a playoff contender than they had over the last few years before Jordan's entry.

As it happens with sports of all kinds, though, injuries can be unkind. In just his third game of the 1985–86 regular season, Jordan suffered a broken foot and had to miss 64 of the remaining 79 games. The Bulls still made the playoffs thanks to Jordan's return. In Game 2 of the Bulls' opening-round series against the Boston Celtics, he set the NBA record for most points in a single playoff game with 63. Unfortunately, the Bulls were swept out of the playoffs again. Two years in the NBA for Michael Jordan, and his team had six playoff losses with zero wins.

This likely motivated Michael Jordan even more. If there is one character trait he is known for, it is his competitiveness. And if there was any worry that his foot injury was going to keep nagging at him moving forward, those worries were quashed quite quickly.

In fact, Jordan's third season in the NBA was a prolific one. While the Bulls fell short of a winning record, Jordan became only the second player in NBA history to score 3,000 points in a single season. He led the league in points per game as well. It was also in this third season that he became the first player in league history to notch 200 steals and 100 blocks in one year. He was a menace on both sides of the ball, which is one of the biggest reasons for his success.

Again, though, when the playoffs rolled around, Chicago was swept in the first round. The Celtics were the culprits once more, and it left Jordan and the Bulls wondering how they could push forward.

Jordan was still doing his part, though, as he led the league in scoring again. He also won his first MVP during that fourth season, as well as the Defensive Player of the Year award. Speaking of defense, the Bulls led the league with the lowest points allowed on the season. This translated to playoff success as well, as the Bulls were able to defeat the Cleveland Cavaliers in the first round before losing to the Detroit Pistons in the second round. In fact, for the next couple of years, this trend would not change. Jordan was a dominant scorer and a great defender, but his team could not figure out how to get around the Pistons when it came to the playoffs.

There are great professional athletes who have never had the fortune of winning a championship. It happens often. However, those athletes are never regarded as the greatest to ever play the game. That title generally requires at least one championship season. Would Jordan and the Bulls find a way through?

The 1990–91 Bulls were looking to change the story. Led by Jordan and a developing Scottie Pippen, the Bulls roared into the playoffs after winning 61 of their 82 regular season games. They defeated the New York Knicks and Philadelphia 76ers before meeting their rivals, the Detroit Pistons, in the Eastern Conference Finals.

Jordan and the Bulls had the answers this time, as they swept the Pistons in four games to advance to the NBA Finals, where they faced Magic Johnson and the Los Angeles Lakers.

Some stars crumble under the pressure of their first championship series, but Michael Jordan had waited long enough to reach this moment. He scored 31 points per game on 56% shooting as the Bulls won the series four games to one. He was awarded the Finals MVP honor, and there are still famous photos and videos of him holding the championship trophy in tears.

What followed over the next two seasons was not a step backwards from the best player in the world. No, he didn't lose focus after winning a title. The Bulls continued to dominate. The 1991–92 season ended with the Bulls atop the league, winning 67 out of 82 games. They defeated Miami,

New York, and Cleveland before conquering Portland to win the championship. Game 1 of that Finals series included a first-half record from Jordan, who scored 35 points by halftime. His performance in the series earned him another Finals MVP nod.

In the 1992–93 season, Jordan and the Bulls had another dominant regular season, but Jordan was not named MVP of the league. Instead, that honor was given to his friend, Charles Barkley of the Phoenix Suns. Jordan was not happy. Thankfully, those two teams met in the NBA Finals, where Jordan could prove the league had made a mistake with their choice. And they had. He averaged 41 points per game as the Bulls beat the Suns in six games. Michael Jordan became the first player to be named Finals MVP three years in a row.

Seven years. Three championships. Multiple records. What was next for Michael Jordan?

Minor league baseball.

This book isn't going to examine Jordan's baseball career in any depth, except to say that he retired from basketball to pursue a baseball career. It did not go very well. After a season and a half of baseball, Jordan returned to the Bulls as they struggled to make the playoffs in the spring of 1995. They did make the playoffs with Jordan's help but were eliminated in the second round by the Orlando Magic.

Maybe he had been away from the game for too long. Perhaps he had made a bad decision by leaving the game. Or, maybe, he just needed some time to get back into the groove.

The Bulls added Dennis Rodman to help on the defensive side of the ball, and the Bulls destroyed the league during the 1995–1996 season. They finished with the best record in NBA history at the time, 72 wins and 10 losses. Their domination continued in the playoffs, where they defeated Miami, New York, Orlando, and Seattle to win another championship, only losing three games along the way. Jordan added another Finals MVP award, earning him the most by any player in NBA history.

The 1996–1997 season ended with yet another championship for Jordan and the Bulls, and it featured one of the more storied moments in Jordan's career. In Game 5 of the Finals, as the series with the Utah Jazz was tied at two games each, Michael Jordan had come down with some sort of illness, possibly the flu, possibly food poisoning. Regardless of the diagnosis, he had to fight through the pain that was coursing through his body to score 35 points and help the Bulls take the series lead. The story goes that Jordan slept as much as possible, waking up only an hour before the game started.

Another championship for the Bulls, another Finals MVP for Michael Jordan.

Oh, and he did it again in 1998, completing another three straight championships and three straight MVP awards, as the Bulls beat the Jazz again.

Michael Jordan would retire again before returning to play a couple more seasons with the Washington Wizards, a team that he partly owned. His final seasons were not as remarkable, as he suffered injuries that made competition difficult. He did cap off his career by becoming the highest scorer in All-Star Game history in 2003, but that record was later broken.

Honestly, it would take an entire book to encapsulate everything that Michael Jordan accomplished and overcame during his career. This chapter didn't even touch his father's murder, or his record in international competitions with Team USA. If you're looking for more inspiration from the player who many consider to be the best of all time, those two topics will get you started in the right direction.

For now, though, it's easy to say that Michael Jordan reached the pinnacle of the sport in every way imaginable. He was tenacious on both sides of the ball, making sure he punished opponents on offense and defense. Most importantly, he was always up for a challenge. He never shied away from an opponent who wanted to challenge him on the court.

He was undefeated in the NBA Finals as a player, meaning that when his team made it to that final series, he always won. His control over the game and his dominance of his opponents is enough to inspire any hopeful player who couldn't make their varsity basketball team on the first try. Hard work and dedication will go far for those who choose to push through adversity.

CHAPTER 3:

MAGIC JOHNSON

There are few individuals in the world of professional sports who have the opportunity to make an impact at the cultural level for millions of people around the world. Sure, there are a couple of players who donate to charities and maybe volunteer a couple of times per year, but then there are players like Magic Johnson, who endured a controversial disease and lived to advocate for others like him.

Let's take a look at the story of Earvin "Magic" Johnson and the positive changes he helped provide to the world around him.

Born in Michigan, Magic Johnson grew up with his father, mother, six siblings, and three half-siblings. His parents both worked very hard, and their hard work made an impression on him. In fact, he used to be teased by kids at school when he helped his father with garbage collecting. He also grew up loving basketball, and he admired players who won multiple championships. With his desire to win, along with a work ethic he developed from his hardworking parents, it seemed he was bound to develop the skills necessary to excel on the basketball court.

As he entered high school, he struggled with racism from the predominately White student body, including his teammates on the basketball team. They wouldn't even pass him the ball at practice. However, he used this experience to grow as a person and learn how to deal with people who did not like him for who he was.

In fact, he'd had a chance to go to a school with students who were more like him, but he was forced out of his comfort zone. If you've ever experienced that, then you know it is difficult and painful. When you are in that difficult situation, your decisions will shape who you are. Magic Johnson made the right choices.

In his sophomore year, he earned that "Magic" nickname from a newspaper reporter after an amazing basketball performance. He continued to improve through his high school career, which culminated with a state championship victory. And with a great high school career, he had plenty of choices when it came to college basketball scholarships.

Instead of picking one of the top-ranked schools, he elected to stay in his hometown and play for the Michigan State Spartans. Johnson chose to major in communications, and his studies came first, rather than all of his focus being on basketball. He was working toward being a television commentator, but basketball was going pretty well, too. In his freshman year, he helped the Spartans reach the Elite Eight before losing to the eventual champions in Kentucky.

Johnson helped the team once more, though, as he led the team in his sophomore year to the NCAA Championship, as the Spartans defeated Larry Bird and the Indiana State Sycamores. Due to Johnson's strong performance in the most-watched college basketball game ever, he attracted the attention of the NBA. His play as a point guard was what earned him so much interest because it is a position often taken by smaller, faster players who could handle the ball well. Johnson had all of those skills, but he was also very large in stature.

In the 1979 draft, the Los Angeles Lakers selected Johnson with the first overall pick. Johnson was added to a Lakers team that already included Kareem Abdul-Jabbar, who would go on to become the leading scorer in NBA history.

In Magic's rookie season, the Lakers finished the season with 60 wins and advanced all the way to the NBA Finals, where they faced the Philadelphia 76ers. The Lakers had a 3-2 lead in the series, but Kareem injured his ankle and could not play in Game 6. Thankfully, Magic Johnson was up to the task, even as a rookie. In Game 6, Magic scored 42 points in the championship-winning game. He was awarded the Finals MVP honors, making him the only rookie in NBA history to earn that distinction.

After a year plagued by injury, Johnson and the Lakers won another championship in 1982, and Johnson earned another Finals MVP. If you're noticing a pattern, it's just that Magic Johnson and the Los Angeles Lakers were really good.

In the 1980s, Magic Johnson and the Lakers won a total of five NBA Championships. Johnson won three Finals MVP honors and three NBA MVP awards. However, things would take a dramatic turn for Johnson in the new decade.

Before the 1991–92 season, things changed dramatically for Johnson as he was going through routine medical exams. It was discovered that Johnson had been infected with HIV, a virus that leads to AIDS, an often-deadly syndrome that was a cultural stigma at the time. Because of his diagnosis and the negative attitude that most people had about it, Johnson announced that he would retire instead of play in the league again.

Rather than playing in the NBA, Johnson decided to dedicate his time and resources to battle against the disease in his body. At that time, it was widely believed that HIV and AIDS only affected same-sex couples, so Johnson's diagnosis and public retirement from the game of basketball opened a lot of eyes to the dangers the disease posed to everyone.

NBA fans recognized that Magic Johnson was still a special player and person. Despite his retirement and his diagnosis, NBA fans voted for Magic Johnson to be a starter in the 1992 NBA All-Star game. This, though, caused distress for NBA players because Johnson playing in the game would expose them to the risk of being contaminated if Johnson suffered some sort of wound while playing.

Johnson ended up playing in that game, scoring 25 points and being voted the All-Star Game MVP. Players from both teams congratulated Johnson on his return, and it was an iconic moment in the history of the sport.

Perhaps because of his performance in that All-Star game, or just because scouts knew how strong of a player Johnson still was even in retirement, he was selected to represent his country in the 1992 Summer Olympics in Barcelona, Spain. That year, the U.S. National Team was known as the "Dream Team" because the roster was made up of NBA stars like Johnson, Larry Bird, and Michael Jordan.

Johnson was not as dominant of a force on this team as he had been for the Lakers in the 80s, but his performances did receive standing ovations from the crowds in Spain. Johnson knew that he was inspiring people, even if he wasn't playing his best basketball. He was making a difference for people that were struggling with the same condition he was. By the way, the Dream Team would go on to win gold medals for the United States.

But, with those appreciative fans in mind, Johnson announced that he would attempt to return to the NBA, despite some of his Olympics teammates thinking that it might not be a good idea for him because of his condition. Johnson ultimately did not return to the league, but he did coach the Lakers for the end of the 1994 season.

Although that was not successful, Johnson made one more return to the NBA as a player, again with the Lakers, during the 1995–1996 season, where he played 32 games and averaged over 14 points per game. The Lakers lost in the first round of the playoffs that spring, but Johnson was happy with his progress on the court.

It would end up being the last time Johnson played in the NBA, ending his career with 17,707 points, 10,141 assists, and 6,559 rebounds. His assists per game average was 11.2, which is the highest by any player to play in the NBA.

Although Johnson's play in the NBA was remarkable, with many considering him to be in the top five players in NBA history, his work off the court during his retirement was just as important. Johnson created a charity event for the United Negro College Fund, which he hosted for 20 years before it was absorbed into the Magic Johnson Foundation.

His foundation helps support ethnically diverse communities, focusing on scholarship, community empowerment, and HIV/AIDS awareness.

When Magic Johnson received his diagnosis back in the early '90s, he could have quietly hidden it from the world, retired from basketball, and lived out his days away from the spectacle that is professional basketball. But Magic Johnson knew that being uncomfortable and being around people who look at you differently, is an opportunity to learn, teach, and change minds. He didn't hide from the world, even when he knew that most people were going to negatively judge him.

He faced his fears on one of the biggest stages this world has to offer, and he did as much as he could to help. He showed others with his condition that there were ways to live and survive. To those without his condition, he explained how to remain safe, and why people like him were not a threat.

If you've ever felt like an outsider to those around you, remember Magic Johnson and the decisions he made when he felt a similar discomfort. Use his story to inspire your next tough decision, even in the faces of those who disapprove of you.

CHAPTER 4:

MAYA MOORE

Becoming a professional athlete is no easy feat. It's a difficult path to trek, a terribly steep mountain to climb. What's even more difficult is the hundreds, thousands of others trying to climb over you, all trying to reach the summit first. It must be even more difficult, then, to decide to climb back down the mountain, even after reaching the summit.

Most athletes wait until they are forcefully pulled down by age, no longer being able to defend their spot at the top. Some athletes, though, decide that their time should be spent elsewhere, attempting to accomplish other goals.

Maya Moore is one of those special athletes who left the summit before she had to but for very honorable reasons.

Let's take a close look at the story of Maya Moore, one of the greatest female basketball players in the history of the sport.

Maya grew up in Missouri, playing basketball with her mom and friends often. She went on to attend a high school in Georgia, where she was already a dominant force on the basketball court. In her four years with Collins Hill High School, her team had a record of 125 wins and three losses. Her team won three state championships and a national championship. Oh, and she also was the state runner-up in the high jump event for her school track team.

With her absolute dominance in basketball established, she elected to play college basketball at Connecticut, one of the best schools in the nation for women's basketball.

Normally, when the freshman player enters the college ranks, their contribution to the team is minimal, as they're playing against other athletes that are three, maybe four years older. Maya Moore forgot that she was a freshman, as she went on to score 678 points that season, the most by any freshman in the school's history.

In Moore's sophomore season, she led the UConn Huskies to an undefeated season of 39 wins and zero losses, which ended in the 2009 National Championship. During that season, she became the fastest player in UConn history to score 1,000 points, averaging 21 points a game during the year.

Just in case anyone thought it was a fluke, Moore helped lead the Huskies to another perfect season in her junior year, with another 39 wins and zero losses, and yet another National Championship victory. Her senior season ended in the Final Four when the Huskies lost to Notre Dame, but Moore had the best season of her career statistically, scoring 22.3 points per game while adding 4.1 assists and 2.2 steals. She also became the first player in UConn history to score 3,000 points.

Overall, Maya Moore finished her college career on a team that had won 150 games and only lost four. She shot 52.5% over her college years, including 40% from the three-point arc.

It was an unprecedented college career, and that college résumé would surely have the attention of the WNBA, the professional basketball league in the United States. Sure enough, with the first overall pick in the 2011 draft, the Minnesota Lynx selected Maya Moore.

In her rookie season, Moore helped the Lynx win more games than any other team that season, culminating in a WNBA Championship. She became only the second player in league history to win the Rookie of the Year and a championship in the same season.

The 2012 season featured more winning matches for the Lynx, as they matched their record from the previous regular season. However, they were defeated in the WNBA Finals by the Indiana Fever. Don't worry, though, because Moore and the Lynx roared back in 2013.

Moore was the scoring leader for the team during the 2013 season and was the first player in league history to lead in both three-point shots made and three-point shooting percentage, and while it seems like those two things should go hand-in-hand, shooting a lot means making a lot, but it can also mean missing a lot.

At the end of the season, the Minnesota Lynx were champions once again, and Maya Moore was selected as the Finals MVP.

In 2014, Moore was scoring even more, notching more than 30 points 12 times in that season. Her dominance resulted in a league MVP award, although her team lost in the conference finals, making it the first time her team had not reached the championship series in four years.

But this is Maya Moore. Of course, she and her team were not done yet! They returned to the WNBA Finals once again in 2015, and they were able to defeat the Indiana Fever three games to two. This included a Game 3 buzzer-beating three-point shot from Moore.

After another championship in 2017, the Minnesota Lynx were not as competitive in 2018, as they barely made the playoffs before being eliminated in the first round.

It seemed as though the championships were going to dry up, but it had been quite a run. Four WNBA titles in the United States, and five gold medals in international competitions, including two Olympic golds in 2012 and 2016—Maya Moore had done a lot of winning in her career. In fact, she had played in multiple leagues around the world (this was necessary to earn a living, given the pay gap in women's basketball). During that time, she also won two

Euro-League Women's championships, a Liga Fementina championship, and three Women's Chinese Basketball Association championships. Everywhere she went, she won. However, she wanted to win somewhere else, still.

After all of the championships around the world, Maya Moore made the shocking decision to step away from basketball, as she wanted to focus more on her ministry work.

Specifically, she wanted to advocate for criminal justice reform, believing that there were punishments that were too harsh on specific individuals. Her efforts, while meant to help all, ultimately focused on one individual by the name of Jonathan Irons, a prisoner she had met almost a decade before through her prison ministry work. Irons had been sentenced to 50 years in prison for burglary and assault charges, crimes that he had committed at the age of 16.

Let's pause here for a moment to reflect. Maya Moore had the world at her feet. She was a dominant force in the WNBA, and that's not even mentioning the fans she had gained internationally, both through her Olympic play and participating in other leagues around the world. She was likely the most well-known women's basketball player in the world. But she put all of that aside to fight for people who needed a second chance at life.

Again, it's important to understand the weight of her decision. She gave up the rest of her basketball career to advocate for people that many have written off. Most people would assume that a prisoner deserves to be there for what they did, but Maya Moore thought they should have another try.

It's difficult to put into words how much bravery her decision must have taken. She ended her professional basketball career for those who needed help, and for Jonathan Irons, it worked. In 2020, a Missouri judge threw out the conviction ruling that kept Jonathan Irons in prison, making him a free man.

Maya Moore saved that man's life. If you asked her whether or not it was worth giving up her basketball career, she would likely tell you that it was. That's the kind of person Maya Moore is. If you're looking for inspiration, and you love the game of basketball, there's no better person to look to than her. She gave up the game she loved, with fans adoring her worldwide, all so she could help a man escape a cruel fate.

CHAPTER 5:

(WARDELL) STEPHEN CURRY

While it is almost impossible for an individual to reach the NBA, the odds are even smaller for multiple individuals from the same family to accomplish the same feat. This story focuses on one member of this special basketball family and how he was able to become one of the best shooters in NBA history.

The Curry family had their first individual enter the NBA when Dell Curry was drafted by the Utah Jazz in 1986. While he played a full career, averaging 11.7 points per game, he was not a superstar in the league. However, he was laying the groundwork for his sons, Stephen and Seth, to make their own paths to the NBA. In fact, Dell would often have his sons on the court during gameday practices, allowing the boys to shoot around with the team, and exposing them to the life they might one day achieve. Stephen was more than interested.

Stephen wanted to follow in his father's footsteps. In fact, as Stephen was playing in high school, he was hoping for a scholarship opportunity to play at Virginia Tech, just as his father did. However, many of the bigger schools in the country were concerned about Stephen's lack of physical size. He was offered opportunities to walk on to some of those bigger schools, but that meant paying for his own schooling, which is very expensive. Because of the lack of offers from the powerhouse schools, he instead considered offers from smaller schools and eventually settled on Davidson College.

In his freshman season, Curry quickly impressed those around him. While he did commit 13 turnovers in his very first game, he rallied and learned from his mistakes. At the end of the season, he was the highest-scoring player in his conference, and only one other freshman in the country scored more than he did: Kevin Durant.

Curry also set the NCAA record for three-point shots made by a freshman with 113. However, his team was ousted from the NCAA tournament in the first round, when they lost to Maryland. Still, Stephen was showered with praise, including several conference awards and honors, and the magazine *Sports Illustrated* gave him an honorable mention. He was also invited to play in the FIBA U19 World Championships, and he helped Team USA win a silver medal in that tournament.

In his sophomore year, Stephen finally reached his full height of six feet, three inches, meaning that he would be even better on the court. Through his scoring prowess, he helped his team go undefeated in conference play, earning another NCAA tournament spot. In this year's tournament, though, Stephen was determined to make it through the first round. However, Davidson College was facing Gonzaga, a team that made it far into the tournament regularly.

Early into the second half, Gonzaga was up by 11 points, but Curry decided that his team was going to win. He scored 30 points in the second half of the game, ending the contest with 40 points total, as Davidson upset Gonzaga by a score of 82-76. It was the first time Davidson had won a game in the NCAA tournament in 38 years.

But Curry and Davidson College were not done yet. Next up, they faced Georgetown, the second seed in their region, and the eighth-ranked team in the country. Again, Davidson fell behind in the first half, sometimes by as many as 17 points, and Curry only had five points going into halftime. But just as he had done in the game before, he decided his team was going to win. He scored 25 points in the second half, for 30 total, and led Davidson to a comeback win over Georgetown, 74-70.

Just to make sure everyone understood that this was not a fluke, Stephen Curry scored 33 points in a win against Wisconsin before narrowly losing to the eventual champions, the Kansas Jayhawks. Still, it was this tournament performance that put the basketball world on notice. Stephen Curry was a natural shooter from anywhere on the court, and he would be coming to the NBA soon.

Still, he remained at Davidson for his junior year, helping the team to an 18-2 conference record, but they did not win the conference championship, nor did they receive an NCAA tournament spot. During one hilarious game that season, Loyola Maryland decided they would try to double-team Stephen Curry for the entire game. Curry finished the game with zero points, but Davidson still won by 30 points.

At the end of his junior year, Stephen decided to enter the NBA draft, where he was selected as the seventh overall pick by the Golden State Warriors. There were still concerns about his size, but Stephen knew he could make up for his lack of physicality by controlling the ball well and shooting with great accuracy. In his rookie year, he proved that he belonged in the league, averaging over 17 points per game, along with four rebounds and nearly six assists per game. He also set the NBA record for most three-point shots made by a rookie. He was the runner-up for Rookie of the Year, but the Warriors didn't make the playoffs that season.

Stephen would not be denied for long, though. As he continued to break personal records and improve his game, he also suffered a few ankle injuries that required surgery. But when Stephen recovered for the 2012–13 season, he partnered up with teammate Klay Thompson to tear up the league with long-range shots. In fact, they became so good at shooting that they earned the nickname, "Splash Brothers," because their shots always splashed into the net from wherever they shot.

Curry set another NBA record with 272 three-point shots made, and he set the record with 53 fewer shots taken than the previous record holder, Ray Allen. After a stronger season from Curry and Thompson, the Warriors made the playoffs as the sixth seed in the Western Conference. He played in 12 playoff games before the Warriors were eliminated, but the three-point shots he made during that time helped him reach 314 on the season, making him the first player in NBA history to make more than 300 in a season.

It's important to pause and remember how Stephen Curry made it to where he was. He was told he was too small by the big colleges, but he proved many of them wrong. He used his shooting skills to make up for the size difference. Now, in the NBA, people were doubting that his ankles would hold up, but he was proving all of them wrong, too. Stephen Curry was taking every opportunity he had, and the skills he'd been working on the whole time were coming in handy for those chances.

Even more importantly, he was revolutionizing the game of basketball. Defenses used to be able to relax as a point guard dribbled up the court to set up an offensive play. Defenders couldn't do that with Stephen Curry, though, because he could score from anywhere. If he was anywhere near the half-court line, then everyone knew he had a chance to score. A player rarely has a big impact on the game, but Stephen Curry was forcing teams to change the way they played defense against him and his team.

In the 2013–14 season, Curry became the ninth player in NBA history to score an average of 24 points and eight assists over the year, and he made his first All-Star appearance. He was the first Warrior to make the special roster since 1995, so it's easy to see that the Warriors were excited about Curry and the things they hoped he would accomplish for them. They made the playoffs again that spring but were eliminated by the Los Angeles Clippers.

However, thanks to a change behind the bench for the 2014–15 season, Curry and the Warriors were playing in a new scheme that featured a faster pace to the team's offense, which gave Curry more chances to score. With more of the scoring on Curry's shoulders, the Warriors had found a winning combination. At the end of the season, the Warriors had won 67 regular season games and were ready for a deep run into the playoffs. To cap it off, Curry and his team defeated LeBron James and the Cleveland Cavaliers to win the NBA Championship. He also set the NBA record for most three-point shots made in a playoff run, which was just another reminder that he loved to shoot the ball.

Now, when a team wins a championship, there is sometimes a lull or slump that follows, because there can be emotional fatigue from being a part of something so dramatic and meaningful. Also, other teams can often plan on how to better adjust to that winning team's strategy. Somehow, neither of these things happened in the 2015–16 season, as the Golden State Warriors went on to win 73 of their 82 regular season games, which was an NBA record. Curry was also voted the league MVP unanimously, which had never happened before. That means that every person who was able to cast a vote for that award voted for Stephen Curry! That's just how good of a season he had. It was undeniable.

The Warriors advanced to the NBA Finals despite an injury that forced Curry to miss many of the team's games. They were ultimately defeated by James and the Cavaliers in seven games.

Some wondered if those injuries would finally catch up to Curry and end the terror he had been inflicting on the league for the last few years. Many probably thought the injuries would slow him down, if not end his career. However, Curry and the Warriors were not done with the league just yet.

In the two seasons that followed, Stephen Curry and the Warriors went on a rampage, which culminated with two consecutive NBA Championship wins. They defeated the Cavaliers in 2017 and 2018, denying LeBron James more championships.

With three championships in four seasons, it was hard to argue that Stephen Curry had been the talented player that sparked a dynasty for the Golden State Warriors. It had been a long time coming. He had to fight through size issues, doubt in his ability to play with bigger opponents, concerns about his ankles and knees, and questions regarding whether or not he matched up against other superstars in the NBA.

Stephen Curry rose to the challenge every time. With dedication and plenty of hard work, Stephen Curry became one of the best shooters in NBA history, proving all of those doubters wrong.

If you are experiencing doubt in your own life, whether it is coming from someone else or maybe from inside you, remember that hard work creates talent, and talent can silence any critic. Look to the story of Stephen Curry and the way he transformed the game of basketball. Not too many players who were denied chances to play at Virginia Tech can say that they revolutionized a sport played by millions of people around the world.

Sometimes, stature isn't a good measure of the impact you can make.

CHAPTER 6:

JIMMY V

Basketball is a game that many people love, and the impact it has on the lives of those who play it can be immense. Sometimes, the impact can come from the camaraderie you experience with your teammates, and you battle together, or it can be from a coach, who might serve as a role model for you as you learn and grow.

This story is about one such coach, who used the remaining years of his life to help impact as many people as possible.

Jimmy Valvano was born in Queens, New York, in 1946, to Rocco and Angelina Valvano. Jimmy grew up as a typical boy in New York, and in high school, he played three sports, though basketball was the sport that garnered him the most attention as he headed off to Rutgers University. As a member of the Scarlet Knights, he led the team to a third-place finish in the NIT, which is a tournament for teams that do not qualify for the NCAA tournament.

After his mildly successful basketball career with Rutgers and graduating from the university with a degree in English, Valvano decided to stay at Rutgers and take a job as the freshman basketball coach. After spending two years in that position, which also involved assisting with the varsity team, Valvano was hired as the head coach for Johns Hopkins University for one season. Though most head coaches wouldn't want to go back to being an assistant,

Valvano left Johns Hopkins to join Connecticut as an assistant coach for two seasons, for the experience on offer compared to a smaller basketball school.

Thankfully, that choice paid off, as Valvano was then hired to be the head coach at Bucknell for three years, and then he went to Iona for five seasons. He is likely most well-known, though, for the 10 years he spent as the head coach of NC State, which is the last school he ever coached.

During his time at NC State, Valvano coached the team to two conference tournament championship victories, and two regular season championships. His crowning jewel, though, came in 1983, when he coached the team to the NCAA Championship. There is a famous video of Coach Valvano reacting to his team making a last-second basket to win the title, and he frantically runs around the court, looking for someone to hug.

He would also lead the team to two more Elite Eight appearances, and while those are not championships, they are indicative of successful seasons. In all, Valvano ended his coaching career with NC State, boasting a record of 209 wins and 114 losses at that school. Unfortunately, his coaching career was cut short by accusations of rule violations from the NCAA. While Valvano was not found to have broken any of the NCAA rules directly, many criticized his program because many of his student-athletes did not do very well in the classroom.

It must have been tough to shoulder that criticism. As a coach, one must care for their players. It's that simple. If a coach does not care, the players will not do their best for that coach. However, some investigators did not find anything wrong with the way Valvano was doing things. One of the NCAA investigators even wrote Valvano a letter to encourage him to keep coaching. The investigator, Dave Didion, wrote, "...I have come to believe that you are one of the best people I have met in intercollegiate athletics and one of the best people I have met period."

Despite this support, there was still pressure from the University for Valvano to step down, so he did. Moving on from his coaching career, he turned to the life of televised sports. Specifically, he got a job working as a broadcaster on ESPN and ABC Sports. One of his first jobs was to report on the first season for the World League of American Football, a league that attempted to compete with the NFL.

While that might not have worked out in the long run, Valvano was a great analyst for NCAA basketball games. It makes sense that he would be able to use his knowledge to help viewers better understand the game on a deeper level. He even won a Cable ACE Award for his broadcasting work.

Valvano also branched out into the realm of motivational speaking, and he toured around the country. He met with hundreds of groups to speak on basketball and success, and he even made appearances on the late-night talk shows of the time, hosted by people such as Johnny Carson and David Letterman.

It seemed like everything was going well for Valvano. Sure, he was no longer coaching NCAA basketball, but he was still around the game, and he got to make a positive impact on his audiences around the country. It was a great time for him, and he was doing everything he could to make it count.

Unfortunately, life had other plans for him. In 1992, Jimmy Valvano was diagnosed with a kind of glandular cancer that can spread to the bones. He didn't know how long he would survive, but the cancer was aggressive, and his chances were not looking very good.

Now, most people who receive a diagnosis like this would likely retire from their job and focus on spending time with family and friends, or maybe even completing a bucket list of things before passing on. Jimmy V didn't do that. He continued to work as an analyst on televised basketball games, and he also began calling for more cancer research to be conducted in the United States.

With that effort in mind, he created the Jimmy V Foundation for Cancer Research, and with every chance he had, he would speak about his battle against cancer, encouraging others to join him in the fight.

Again, he didn't want to go quietly. He wanted to give hope to the people who needed it more than he did. He wanted to inspire them to continue forward in the face of death.

Because of his bravery and courage in such a difficult situation, ESPN honored Valvano by awarding him the Arthur Ashe Award at the ESPY Awards ceremony in March 1993. On that night, Valvano needed help getting up the stairs and onto the stage. The crowd cheered and cried as he approached the podium to make his speech.

One of his statements included a list of three things he thought should be accomplished every day. This is what Jim Valvano said:

"Number one is laugh. You should laugh every day. Number two is 'think'. You should spend some time in thought. And number three is, you should have your emotions moved to tears...

...If you laugh, you think, and you cry, that's a full day. That's a heck of a day. You do for that seven days a week, you're going to have something special."

Less than two months after his speech at the ESPY Awards, Jim Valvano passed away. He can no longer give speeches and inspire those around him. However, with the words on his tombstone, he still gives that great advice: "Take time every day to laugh, to think, to cry."

Even in death, Jim Valvano wanted the world to take in his words and live better lives.

Jim Valvano's foundation continues to raise funds for cancer research. According to the website of his foundation, they have raised over $60 million for blood cancer research, $66 million for pediatric cancer research, $30 million for breast cancer research, and $26 million for lung cancer research.

Try to remember that life is precious and that even when all of the odds seem against you, and there doesn't look like there is a way to get anything positive out of a situation, you still have an opportunity to make a positive difference for those around you. Jimmy Valvano found a way to give as much as he could, and his actions have reverberated throughout time, even today, 30 years after his passing.

CHAPTER 7:

CHRIS PAUL'S 61

Everyone knows that the path to becoming an NBA player is extremely narrow, and becoming an NBA superstar is ever rarer. Players who make it to that peak often get help from those around them, whether it be friends, teammates, coaches, or family members. We're going to take a look at one of the best point guards to ever play the game and examine how his family helped him reach that peak in his career. We'll also talk about one specific game in this player's career, which he dedicated to his family member.

This story is about Chris Paul, who many consider to be one of the most talented players to ever walk onto an NBA court. But let's start at the beginning.

Chris was born in North Carolina, where he grew up playing basketball with his father, brother, and grandfather. Chris was very close to his family, but he considered his grandfather to be his best friend.

If you have many family members around you, then you understand how important support from family can be. Sometimes you grow to trust each other enough that you can help one another through troubling times. Family members can support each other in ways that friends cannot. Chris had that support, and it would aid in his trek to the NBA.

His early basketball days, including his first two years in high school, were no indication that he was on the verge of becoming one of the best. Chris played junior varsity as a freshman and sophomore, but when he played for his varsity high school team, things began to change drastically. During his junior year, Chris impressed with 25 points per game, including five assists and four steals on average. With play at such a high level, Chris led his high school team to the state semifinals. That summer, he was the point guard on a travel team that went on to win the national championship tournament for players under the age of 17.

During his senior year, tragedy struck for Chris and his family. Chris' grandfather, Nathaniel Jones, was killed in a senseless attack by a group of robbers. He was 61 years old when his life was taken from him, and young Chris Paul was looking for a way to pay tribute to him. His aunt suggested scoring 61 points for him, and Chris agreed that it would be a great story, but that was a lot of scoring.

Still, Chris was determined, and family can be a strong motivator. In his next game, Chris went to work, his parents unaware of what he had planned. The first quarter was average, but in the second quarter, he scored 24 points. His team pulled ahead in the third, giving Chris an opportunity to go for the points he needed.

With 59 points to his name, he drove to the basket hard late in the contest. As he went for the layup he needed, he was fouled hard, but the shot went in. He had 61 points, and a free throw coming up. There was enough time left in the game for Chris to break the state record of 67 points, and this free throw would put him within striking distance.

As Chris was passed the ball and prepared to take his free throw, though, he already knew what he was going to do. The ball left his hands, floated through the air, and missed completely before bouncing out of bounds. Chris' coach subbed him out, and when Chris reached the bench, he burst into tears. One point for each year of his grandfather's life. The tribute was complete.

The story made national headlines when it happened. Few people assumed, though, that it would only be the first of many headlines featuring the talented player that is Chris Paul. He completed his senior season with a scoring average of 30.8 points, 9.5 assists, 6 steals, and 5.9 rebounds. He was named a McDonald's All-American, and *The Charlotte Observer* awarded him the title of North Carolina's Mr. Basketball.

With a strong high school career, Chris was able to attend Wake Forest University and play on their basketball team, where he immediately made an impact, even as a freshman. In fact, Chris set several school records for a freshman player, including the most assists, steals, free throws, and best three-point shooting percentage. Because of his strong play that year, he helped his team reach the Sweet 16 of the NCAA tournament.

Chris Paul helped his team even further during his sophomore season when it earned the number one ranking in the country, which had never happened to that school before. They beat some of the best teams in the country, including Duke and North Carolina.

However, Chris made a poor decision during the final regular season game, when he punched an opposing player in the groin, earning him a one-game suspension. It was an incident that put Chris in a negative light around the world of basketball, but he proved that it was not a situation that would happen again. At the end of the season, he was named First Team All-America. Shortly after, he announced that he would be entering the NBA draft.

Thankfully, many NBA teams believed that Chris Paul would not develop into a dirty player after his suspension during the previous season. He was drafted with the fourth overall pick by the New Orleans Hornets in 2005, beginning his NBA career.

Perhaps the Hornets had done their research on Chris Paul and learned about the story of his grandfather, and how Chris had dedicated that high school game to his lost family member. Doing a good thing in the world does not always mean you'll reap the benefits of it immediately. Put goodness into the world, and goodness will return to you.

But would the Hornets regret their pick?

Definitely not.

During his rookie season with the Hornets, Paul led all rookies in points, steals, assists, and double-double games. Not only did he lead all rookies in steals, but he became only the second rookie in NBA history to lead the entire league in the category. Paul was named NBA Rookie of the Year, falling only one vote short of winning the award unanimously.

His sophomore season featured more scoring and more assists, but Paul missed 18 games with injury issues. However, he wouldn't let this issue slow him down, as he was determined to continue rising to the ranks of NBA stardom.

During his third season, Chris was selected to play in the NBA All-Star Game for the first time, and the game was set to take place in New Orleans, where his hometown fans would be particularly excited to see him perform. It was a special event, and it put Chris and the Hornets on the radar of the national media. It also helped that the team around him was improving as well. At the end of the season, the Hornets found themselves in second place in their conference, meaning they would play their first-round playoff series with home-court advantage.

After making his playoff debut and scoring 35 points, his team went on to defeat the Dallas Mavericks in five games. They would be eliminated in the next round by the San Antonio Spurs, but Paul was excited about the team's progress.

In the 2008–09 season, Paul would collect the NBA record for most games in a row with at least one steal, as he had played 106 games in a row with a steal. Paul's game continued to excel, but the Hornets were not doing as well around him. As a result, the Hornets were eliminated from the playoffs in the first round.

At this point in Chris Paul's career, it's easy to see that he was a special player. The story from his high school days proved to be a good omen for his future, despite his suspension at the college level. However, Chris Paul had not found a ton of playoff success. Would he be able to find the next level of his career?

Unfortunately, another injury would set Chris back, as he only played 45 games in the 2009–10 season, and the Hornets missed the playoffs.

It's important to note that injuries in the sport of basketball can be quite detrimental, even when they seem minute in comparison to injuries in other sports. The game is played on a hard floor, and that can be tough on the human body.

In the 2010–11 season, Paul gave everything he had, helping the Hornets make the playoffs once again, where they faced the Los Angeles Lakers. Unfortunately, despite some impressive performances, Paul's Hornets were eliminated in six games. After that series, Paul decided it was time to move on from the team that drafted him.

After being traded to the Los Angeles Clippers, Paul's control of the basketball would prompt many around the world of basketball to call this Clippers team "Lob City," because Paul would often make alley-oop passes to his teammates for easy dunks. His superstar teammates in Blake Griffin and DeAndre Jordan made the Clippers a serious team to contend with, but they lost in the second round that year to the San Antonio Spurs.

After the second-round exit, what followed in Chris Paul's career was a stretch of three seasons that all included poor playoff performances, including a second-round loss to the Oklahoma City Thunder in 2014. That series featured a Game 5 where Paul made a few critical mistakes late in the game to hand the Thunder the victory and the series lead.

But Chris Paul did not shy away from the criticism. When reporters asked what went wrong, he had two words for an answer: "It's me."

Players who understand that their errors are their own fault will often find a way to repair those errors, learn from them, and improve for the next time they are in that situation. Chris Paul has continued to compete at the highest level, playing a couple more seasons with the Clippers before moving on to the Houston Rockets for two seasons. In fact, his first season with the Rockets included his first appearance in the Conference Finals, where his team lost to the Golden State Warriors, and where Paul suffered a hamstring injury and missed Games 6 and 7 of the series. Golden State won them both and won the series.

Paul played a season with the Oklahoma City Thunder, which featured another first-round exit before landing with his current team, the Phoenix Suns. In the 2021 NBA playoffs, Paul made his first trip to the final series, but his team would lose to the Milwaukee Bucks. With that loss, Paul became the holder of a dubious record, being the only NBA player in history to be part of four teams that have taken a two-game lead in a series before losing that series.

Despite the doubts circling him and his potential legacy as he reaches the later stages of his career, Chris Paul has continued to perform at high levels. In late 2022, Paul reached the milestone of 11,000 assists, becoming only the third player in NBA history to reach the mark. He also has accumulated enough steals to rank third all-time. In fact, he's the only NBA player to lead the league in steals in six different seasons.

Chris Paul may not have many years of basketball left in him, but he has left no doubt that he is one of the best to ever play the game. He has the talent, creativity, and intellect required to excel on the court, and he has shown those abilities for several years. Whether or not he gets a championship before his career comes to an end is unknown. If he does, it will be well deserved. If he does not, fans of basketball will know that he did everything in his power to win.

Just as he dedicated a game to his grandfather and reached the pinnacle he was shooting for back then, he has a few more chances to reach the pinnacle of being an NBA champion. Here's hoping he is successful.

CHAPTER 8:

KOBE BRYANT

While it's easy to see professional athletes on television and be envious of the often-exuberant lives they live, many often forget that reaching the highest levels of a sport requires dedication in the form of thousands and thousands of work hours.

The invention of social media has allowed fans to see more of an athlete's life than ever before, including some of that hard work. One of the biggest names in the sport to demonstrate the tireless training required to be great was Kobe Bryant.

Let's take a look at the story of Kobe's historic basketball career, along with the life he led to reach the milestones he did.

Kobe Bryant was born in 1978 in Philadelphia, and by the age of three, he was playing basketball. After all, it ran in his family. Both his father and his uncle were professional basketball players themselves, so it was only natural that Kobe was following the same path so early.

After Kobe's father, Joe, retired from the NBA, he moved his family to Italy, where Joe would play a few more years of professional basketball. During that time, Kobe began to take basketball quite seriously. In fact, Kobe's grandfather would often send tapes of NBA games to Kobe so he could study them.

Studying game film usually doesn't happen until a player is on a competitive team with coaches who can guide their players through the process. Kobe was not going to wait for a coach's permission to learn more about the game. He wanted to devour anything and everything related to the sport, even when he couldn't be on the court to play or practice.

His family moved back to Philadelphia a year before Kobe would be attending high school, so he ended up at Lower Merion High School, located in a Philadelphia suburb. Quickly, he gained attention for his basketball skills. He made the varsity team as a freshman, and he even played every position on the court throughout the year, but the team did not perform well. Still, experience at each position can go a long way in helping a player understand how everything happens on the court.

The team's fortunes would change as Kobe continued to hone his skills and mature. In his junior year, Bryant was named the Pennsylvania Player of the Year, as he averaged over 31 points per game. Soon after, the major basketball universities from around the country came calling, but Kobe was also being influenced by another player's decision.

That very summer, as Kobe was preparing to begin his senior season, a good, young player named Kevin Garnett, who had just finished his high school career, had just been selected in the first round of the NBA draft. Kobe saw what was possible, but he still had a season to decide.

In that senior high school season, Kobe Bryant helped his team win a state championship victory for the first time in 53 years. At the end of that season, he was the leading scorer from Southeastern Pennsylvania, scoring more points than Wilt Chamberlain did.

After receiving several accolades, including a *USA Today* All-USA First Team nomination, Bryant ultimately decided to enter the NBA draft. After working out in Los Angeles, the Lakers knew that they wanted to draft Bryant, but kept it a secret until they secured a deal with the Charlotte Hornets for their first-round pick. So, with the 13th overall pick, the Hornets selected Kobe Bryant, who was promptly traded to the Los Angeles Lakers.

When Kobe was traded to Los Angeles, he actually needed his parents to co-sign on his contract with the team because he was still 17 and it was illegal for a minor to enter into a legal contract.

During his rookie season, Bryant mostly came off the bench for his minutes. However, as the season progressed, he eventually earned one of the starting positions, becoming the youngest player in league history to do so. His minutes on the floor also increased as the season continued. Bryant's rookie season ended quite roughly, as he missed several shots at the end of Game 5 versus the Utah Jazz in the second round of the playoffs. The Jazz eliminated the Lakers in that game, but many credited Bryant for having the courage to take those shots, even as a rookie.

As his sophomore season began, his minutes increased once more. With that came an increase in scoring production. Through his new role on the team, Bryant impressed the basketball world and became the youngest player in league history to be voted as an All-Star Game starter.

His third year marked the first time he started every game for the team as the guard, and his skills had many around the basketball world comparing him to some of the all-time greats. However, the team did not make it past the second round again.

At this point, you've seen that Kobe Bryant has been willing to put in the work necessary to be a success. If you understand that Kobe Bryant was one of the hardest workers in terms of practice and study, you'd know that it was only a matter of time before he would bring a championship to his team. It also helped when legendary coach Phil Jackson came to the team in 1999.

Using the same offense from his Chicago Bulls teams of the '90s, Coach Jackson helped Kobe Bryant and center Shaquille

O'Neal become legitimate superstars. Between those two amazing players, the Los Angeles Lakers were able to defeat the Indiana Pacers to capture the NBA Championship.

Not wanting to be outdone by anyone other than himself, Bryant increased his scoring in the 2000–01 season by six points, nearly matching his high school output. However, tensions bubbled between him and O'Neal, the star center of the team. Perhaps because of these off-court issues, the Lakers won 11 fewer games in the regular season compared to the season before.

Many predicted that the Lakers were not the same contenders as they were last year, but Kobe Bryant was determined to prove them wrong. As the playoffs began, the Lakers got red-hot. They swept the Portland Trail Blazers in the first round, not losing a single game as they advanced. To match their previous series, they also defeated the Sacramento Kings without losing a game. This series also featured a 48-point performance from Bryant in Game 4.

In the Conference Finals, the Lakers continued their winning ways by sweeping the San Antonio Spurs, again not losing a single game. It was another trip to the Finals for Bryant, O'Neal, and the Lakers.

Their opponent this year was the Philadelphia 76ers, and many early predictions unsurprisingly thought the Lakers would continue cruising to another championship, as they had just won 11 straight to reach the Finals.

In Game 1, though, the 76ers shocked the Lakers and the world by winning in overtime. Suddenly, the narrative shifted. Perhaps the Lakers had run out of steam against a team that may have cracked the code.

Just kidding! The Lakers won the next four games in a row to capture their second straight championship. Bryant's teammate, Shaquille O'Neal, told the world that Kobe Bryant was the best player in the game, silencing the critics of their tumultuous friendship for the time being.

With two championships by the age of 22, things were looking up for Bryant, though he was still not selected for the first-team honors. For the 2001–02 season, the Lakers refused to let go of their dominance. They ended the regular season as the second seed in their conference behind the Sacramento Kings. As the playoffs began, Bryant and the Lakers defeated the Blazers and Spurs, only losing one game along the way, setting up a conference final between them and the Kings, who had home-court advantage.

The series went to seven games, each team winning three along the way. The seventh game was in Sacramento, and a road team had not won a Game 7 of a conference final in 20 years. And, of course, the two teams needed overtime to find a winner. After a grueling battle, the Lakers emerged victorious behind clutch free throws from Bryant and O'Neal in the overtime session. They were heading to their third-straight NBA Finals, in an attempt to defend their championship once more.

Just as he had been for the last couple of years, Kobe Bryant was a force to be reckoned with once more in these Finals against the New Jersey Nets. Bryant averaged over 26 points per game on 51% shooting. Overall, he scored 25% of the team's points in the Finals as the Lakers swept the Nets in four straight games. Kobe Bryant had become the first player in NBA history to win three championships by the age of 23.

Most notably, Kobe Bryant had become known and feared around the league for how well he was playing in the fourth quarter during that playoff run. It was a far cry from his rookie season when he had missed all of those shots as his team was eliminated. Instead, he had worked hard and flipped the script, showing the world that he was a clutch player, meaning that he could make difficult plays at crucial moments in the game.

He was a competitor in every sense of the word. He was selected to compete for the United States at the 2008 Olympics in Beijing, a team compiled of many NBA stars in an attempt to replicate the Dream Team of the '90s. Bryant took the challenge seriously, making it clear that he was going to win.

In USA's way were the defending champions, Spain. One of Spain's best players at the time was Pau Gasol, who happened to be Kobe Bryant's teammate at the Los Angeles Lakers. Kobe made it clear to his USA teammates that he was determined to win against anyone, even his teammate from the Lakers.

Dwayne Wade and LeBron James both recall Bryant telling them before the game that he was going to run through Pau Gasol on the first play of the game. When he said "run through," Bryant meant that he was going to run into Gasol on purpose, rather than go around him to defend the player with the ball.

His teammates didn't believe him when he said it.

They should have.

As the Spain players moved the ball around the court, Gasol set up a screen to make Bryant's path to the ball much longer, but Bryant didn't care. The sound of the impact was immense as Bryant's shoulder went directly into Gasol's chest, sending him sliding on his back along the court.

Bryant delivered the message not to Gasol but to his Team USA teammates. He was not going home without a gold medal.

Team USA would go on to win that gold medal, beating Spain twice in the process. Bryant and Team USA would win another gold medal in the 2012 Olympics as well.

On top of that, Bryant and Gasol would win NBA Championships in 2009 and 2010, thereby cementing Bryant's resume as one of the best players in NBA history. Five championships over a career can do that to a player.

Bryant retired in 2016 at the age of 37, leaving behind a slew of NBA records that place him among the best to ever play the game. As an example, he was the first player in league history to tally 30,000 points and 6,000 assists.

Unfortunately, a couple of years after his retirement, Kobe Bryant passed away in a helicopter crash.

Kobe Bryant's legacy as a fierce competitor lives on, despite his life being cut short. The All-Star Game MVP award now bears Bryant's name, showing just how much of an impact Bryant had on the entire sport of basketball, not just the Lakers. He had transcended basketball. And he did it all with dedication, hard work, and passion.

CHAPTER 9:

LEBRON JAMES

Where you grow up can sometimes be an important part of who you are. If you stay in the same neighborhood for a large portion of your life, it can imprint itself as a living thing in your mind, something you care about, just like you care about members of your family. It becomes a part of who you are, and you often have pride associated with that place because of that attachment.

When that happens, you usually want to do everything you can for your hometown. You want to bring joy to those around you, especially if your town has fallen on hard times, as happens throughout history.

The story of LeBron James revolves around the state of Ohio, where James grew up. Ohio, in recent history, has been a difficult place to be a sports fan, especially when it comes to football and basketball. Let's examine the story of LeBron James from the beginning to see how he strived to bring some happiness to the region he calls home.

LeBron James did not grow up in a stable family situation, as his father was not part of his upbringing. His mother also struggled to find work and housing when LeBron was a young child. Because of these difficulties, she allowed her son to move in with a local youth football coach and his family. This adoptive family introduced LeBron to basketball, beginning his journey to the NBA.

He began playing travel basketball in middle school, where his team excelled. He and his friends from that team wanted to attend high school together to continue their winning ways, so they elected to enroll at St. Vincent-St. Mary, a Catholic school with mostly White students. People in the neighborhood were not happy with the boys' decision, as they wanted LeBron and his friends to play at the local high school instead.

Still, LeBron kept his focus on basketball, and his focus paid off, even during his freshman year. He averaged 21 points per game as his team, the Fighting Irish, finished the season undefeated and state champions.

The talented young player had already attracted the attention of NBA scouts and national media. During his sophomore season, the team played some of their home games at the University of Akron because tickets to see LeBron were in high demand.

Imagine the pressure at 16 years old of people from around the country already celebrating you as the number one pick in the NBA draft two years in the future! Coupled with his troubled childhood, there was a worry that LeBron would lose his way and make some poor decisions.

However, LeBron James just kept his focus on basketball.

His sophomore year ended with another state championship, and as LeBron grew in height, the excitement from the national media continued to grow with him. During his junior season, in fact, he became the first non-senior high school student to make the cover of *Sports Illustrated* magazine.

His team lost in the state championship at the end of his junior year, but LeBron had his sights set higher than high school basketball. He petitioned the NBA to change their eligibility rules to let him enter the NBA draft before his senior year in high school, but his petition was denied.

Imagine being so good at something that you are ready to enter competition against adults a decade older than you, and you haven't even finished high school yet. The pressure must have been immense.

It turns out that the pressure was getting to LeBron a little bit, as reports surfaced that he had been smoking marijuana on occasion to deal with the stress. This was a much bigger deal back in the early 2000s, so many began watching LeBron with a much closer lens.

Would he crack under the strain that no high school senior should have to endure?

During that senior year, James and his team played some of the best teams around the country. Many of those games were also televised nationally. Even the most casual basketball fan was aware of LeBron James, and everyone was impatiently waiting for him to enter the NBA. In the meantime, LeBron got in a little more trouble, this time with laws concerning his amateur status. High school students are not allowed to receive compensation for their play, but there were plenty of businesses looking to exploit his popularity for their own needs.

He received a two-game suspension as a result. It could have been worse, as he was almost barred from playing the rest of the season.

For good measure, LeBron scored 52 points in his first game after being suspended. Then, he led his team to one more state championship to end his high school career.

The hype around LeBron was building to a fever pitch, so it was no surprise when he was drafted first overall by the team nearest to his hometown, the Cleveland Cavaliers.

What unfolded over the next couple of seasons was pretty much exactly as expected. LeBron James quickly established himself as a dominant player in the league, winning the Rookie of the Year award in 2004, and bringing the Cavaliers to their first-ever NBA Finals in the 2006–07 season. However, he was unable to help the team win a championship. It didn't help things that James also won

NBA MVP awards in 2009 and 2010. After six years in the NBA, James failed to win an NBA Championship with the Cavaliers. Since he did not like the direction that the team was taking, he began looking for another team to join.

Buzz around the league was massive as LeBron was shopping for a team that could afford him and instantly become a contender. After lots of speculation, LeBron announced his new team in a nationally-televised event called *The Decision*. The move to put this moment on television drew some negative reactions from critics of LeBron. After all, players switch teams all the time. But, in LeBron's defense, not all of those players who go to new teams are LeBron James.

Regardless, LeBron played four seasons with the Miami Heat, along with superstars Dwayne Wade and Chris Bosh. In those four seasons in Miami, the Heat won two NBA Championships. LeBron was awarded the league MVP award twice, and he was named the Finals MVP for both of those championship years.

But it was likely that something was eating at LeBron. After all, he had won two NBA Championships, but he had reached that pinnacle with a team that wasn't his own. Maybe he remembered his years growing up in Ohio, realizing that he had left something behind in pursuit of glory. Or maybe he was just homesick.

Whatever it was, it got to LeBron. At the end of the 2014 season, LeBron James opted to leave Miami and re-sign with the Cleveland Cavaliers once more. Perhaps he believed that he finally had the tools necessary to win a championship for the city of Cleveland and the state of Ohio. In his first return season with the Cavaliers, James played an injury-shortened regular season of 69 games, averaging over 25 points per game, along with 7.4 assists and 6 rebounds.

In the playoffs, the Cavaliers with LeBron at the helm were determined to win. They opened up their playoff campaign by sweeping the Boston Celtics in four games, then took on the Chicago Bulls. LeBron and company continued their winning ways in the second round, winning the series in six games. In the Eastern Conference Finals, the Cavaliers swept the Atlanta Hawks, setting up a Finals matchup between Cleveland and Golden State.

Unfortunately, in those Finals, two of LeBron's teammates, Kyrie Irving and Kevin Love, were struggling with injuries. LeBron did his best to carry the offense for his team, but the Cavaliers were ultimately defeated in six games.

It was deflating for the city of Cleveland, but LeBron was not ready to give up.

As the 2015–16 season began, the Cavaliers were dealing with off-court issues, including their coach being fired in the middle of the year. Some speculated that LeBron James had ordered the coach to be fired, and that drew criticism from media pundits around the league. While distractions can often cause a team to perform poorly on the court, LeBron and the Cavaliers found a way to push through. At the end of the season, the Cavaliers had won 57 games to capture the top seed in the Eastern Conference.

In the first round, Cleveland faced the Detroit Pistons, but made quick work of their opponent, winning all four games to sweep the round. Moving to the second round, they again swept their opponent, the Atlanta Hawks. Eight games, eight wins for the Cavaliers, and they were halfway to an NBA Championship.

The Eastern Conference Finals against the Toronto Raptors proved to be more of a challenge for LeBron and his hometown team. Ultimately, the Cavaliers won the series in six games, setting up a rematch against the Golden State Warriors, the team that had defeated the Cavaliers in the Finals last year.

Even worse, the Warriors were coming off a record-setting regular season where they won 73 games. In Game 1, the Cavaliers were torched by the Warriors, who won the game by 15 points. Game 2 was worse, as the Cavaliers lost by 33 points.

The city of Cleveland, with LeBron James fighting for them in the Finals, was likely more than distraught at this point in the series. Down two games to the best regular season team in history, things were not looking good for the Cavaliers.

However, when the series came back to Cleveland, LeBron delivered a 30-point victory, making the series two games to one.

Game 4 in Cleveland, then, would have been a hopeful moment for the city. But Golden State was not ready to let the Cleveland sports curse die. Stephen Curry scored 38 points to help his team earn a 3-1 lead in the series.

Still, LeBron James refused to let his team be defeated again. In Game 5, the Cavaliers went into Golden State territory and put on a show. LeBron James and Kyrie Irving scored 41 points each, and the Cavaliers won the game 112-97.

The series was now 3-2 in favor of the Golden State. Cleveland still needed to win the final two games to win the championship. Game 6 featured another 41 points from LeBron James, and the Cavaliers used encouragement from their home crowd to win Game 6, 115-101.

Game 7, the final game of the series, was a close matchup. But there is one key moment that will live on in NBA history, and of course, it involves LeBron James. With two minutes left in the game, the score was 89-89. Every possession mattered. That's why, when Kyrie Irving missed a floating shot and the ball was turned over to Andre Iguodala and Stephen Curry for a fast break chance, LeBron did not give up on the play.

Iguodala passed the ball to Curry, who returned it right back to Iguodala. As he caught the pass and drove to the basket for a layup, LeBron James stormed back up the court to do anything he could. As Iguodala left his feet to lay the ball into the basket, James jumped from behind him, meeting the ball just before it touched the backboard and blocking it from reaching the hoop.

It was the moment of the entire series. LeBron James was not going to be denied. The entire crowd dulled, understanding what they had just witnessed. Golden State did not score for the remainder of the game, and the Cleveland Cavaliers went on to win 93-89. Finally, an NBA Championship for the city of Cleveland, hand delivered by LeBron James.

He didn't get one the first time around. But he didn't abandon the city. He came back, understanding that Ohio, Cleveland, and Akron had given him so much. He wanted to give it back. And he did.

LeBron James' career since that championship victory has had many individual successes. He took the Cavaliers back to the Finals twice more, but both ended in losses to the Warriors. After those two years, he left in free agency to join the Los Angeles Lakers, one of the most storied teams in NBA history.

After a couple of seasons of injuries, James and the Lakers won a championship in 2020, defeating the Miami Heat in six games. With the victory, James became the first player in basketball history to win a Finals MVP with three different teams.

Since then, James has spent the remaining years of his career breaking records. He became the first player in NBA history to score 30,000 points, 10,000 rebounds, and 9,000 assists. He also became the league's all-time leading scorer in February of 2023.

It has been a career of greatness for LeBron James, all of which began back in Akron, Ohio, where he learned to play the game. He did not abandon his hometown, even if he couldn't bring them a championship right away. He made some mistakes along the way, but he will ultimately go down as one of the best players in the history of the game. LeBron James showed that where you grow up is important, and he did that by winning those living there a championship, and by starting a charitable foundation. The LeBron James Family Foundation helped create an elementary school for struggling students in Akron, along with a housing complex and medical center.

He's given much back to the city that helped set him on the path to success. He did not forget his roots.

CHAPTER 10:

SHAQUILLE O'NEAL

There are many ways an NBA player can make a positive impact on the world around them, even after their career is over. Some players donate time or money to make a difference for those around them. Other players, like Shaquille O'Neal, find more creative ways to help. First, though, let's examine the NBA career of Shaquille O'Neal, or Shaq for short.

Short, though, was something that Shaq was not. Both of his parents were just over six feet tall, but he grew even more. He was six feet, six inches tall by the age of 13, but he was not playing organized basketball. Shaq would shoot around at the local Boys and Girls Club, but that would also come to an end when his family had to move to Germany for his stepfather's military service.

Once he returned to the US, though, Shaq was ready to show that he was a natural basketball talent. Playing at Robert G. Cole High School in San Antonio, Texas, he led his team to a near-perfect record for three seasons, ending with a state championship during his senior year. He also holds the state record for rebounds in a season, with 791.

With his great high school performance, Shaq went on to play college basketball at Louisiana State University, where he also studied business. After three successful years there, he moved on to the NBA. Although he left the university early to start his professional basketball career, he would continue his studies later on and complete his degree.

With the first overall pick in the 1992 draft, the Orlando Magic selected Shaquille O'Neal, and he did not wait to make an impact on the league. To begin the regular season, Shaq became the first player in league history to be named NBA Player of the Week during their first week of playing in the league. Throughout the season, Shaq helped the Magic improve their record by winning 20 more games than the previous one, though they did not make the playoffs. Shaq was named Rookie of the Year, as he averaged over 23 points per game on 56.2% shooting, along with nearly 14 rebounds per game. He was also voted to be a starter at the All-Star Game, the first rookie to earn that honor since Michael Jordan did it in 1985.

In his second season with Orlando, Shaq increased his scoring to over 29 points per game, and he led the NBA with a shooting percentage of 60%. However, he struggled during his first playoff series, as the Indiana Pacers defeated the Magic easily.

Despite the tough playoff outing, Shaq was still improving his game, and he went on to lead the NBA in scoring, as he averaged 29.3 points per game in his third season. The Magic won 57 regular season games and were much more prepared for the playoffs this time around. In the first round, the Magic defeated the Boston Celtics, then toppled the Chicago Bulls in the second. This set them up for a rematch with the Pacers in the Conference Finals. Shaq and his team delivered, earning his first trip to the NBA Finals. His team would ultimately lose in four straight games to the Houston Rockets, but Shaq had learned a lot from his deep playoff run.

Shaq missed much of his next season with injuries, but he still helped the Magic reach the playoffs. They were eliminated by the 72-win Chicago Bulls, though, before they could reach the Finals.

Going into the 1996–97 season, Shaq was a free agent. Because of many disagreements with the head coach in Orlando, he began looking for another team to join. In the meantime, he was named to the US Men's Basketball Team to compete in the 1996 Olympic Games in Atlanta. His team would go on to win the gold medal in the event, and he also signed a contract to play with the Los Angeles Lakers. It was a big summer for Shaq, who was also making quite a large amount of money from endorsements, as many top athletes do.

After a couple of seasons with the Lakers that produced decent results but no championships, things began to look up when Kobe Bryant was drafted by the team. It also helped when Phil Jackson agreed to coach. During the 1999–2000 season, Shaq was voted as the league MVP, only falling one vote shy of being the first-ever unanimously selected MVP. The Lakers would also go on to win the NBA championship three years in a row, and O'Neal was named the Finals MVP for each of those championships. He also set the record for the highest points percentage by a center in the history of the NBA Finals.

However, things would boil over in Los Angeles as Shaq and Kobe could not find a way to peacefully exist together. Shaq was traded to Miami instead, where he was able to prove that his dominance was not reliant on Kobe Bryant. In the 2006 playoffs, Shaq led the Miami Heat to their first-ever Finals appearance, where they defeated the Dallas Mavericks.

O'Neal would finish his career with various teams, including Boston, Cleveland, and Phoenix. To date, he still holds many NBA records, although some are not the kind one likes to have. For example, he's the only NBA player to miss 11 free throws in a single game, without making at least one. On the positive side, though, Shaq was the NBA leader in shooting percentage for 10 seasons, which is a record.

While O'Neal had quite the hold on American media and pop culture, including a music career, an acting career, and more, where he truly made the most difference was in his charity work.

Through his foundation, which bears his name, schools around the country received more than $320,000 in funding for sports equipment and transportation services during the pandemic.

O'Neal also helps students with annual programs like "Shaq-to-School," a giveaway program for students in Los Angeles and Las Vegas. Primary and secondary school students from low-income areas receive backpacks full of supplies and a new pair of shoes for the upcoming school year. Aside from the 5,000 students who benefited from this program in those two cities, the program also shipped 250,000 school supplies across the country, helping students everywhere.

If you can't tell, Shaq likes to put his name in his programs, hence this next program, Shaq-a-Claus. Every year since 1997, Shaq puts on the Santa Claus hat during the holidays and donates thousands of toys, clothing, meals, and more to needy kids around the country. In 2021, events held in five different states impacted 1,300 kids in need.

Shaquille is also a big supporter of organizations that helped him in his younger years. Two of them, specifically, are the

Boys and Girls Clubs of America, which provide after-school programs for students, and The General Car Insurance company. Shaq has helped several Boys and Girls Club locations around the country by refurbishing equipment like basketball courts or playgrounds, and he even helped open the first Club in Henry County, Georgia, which included a $1 million renovation to the building, allowing more than 300 students to participate in activities with a music studio, computer lab, and gymnasium.

As for The General, which is a lower-end, more accessible car insurance company, Shaq has been a spokesperson for them for quite a long time. Although many athletes of Shaq's caliber are often recruited by larger organizations who can pay more for their services, Shaq has remained dedicated to The General. Shaq has said that The General was there for him when he was a young driver and needed insurance.

It's these kinds of people, the ones that remember those who helped along the way, who can make a true difference in the world.

Shaquille O'Neal is not a perfect person, and this book does not argue that he is. He dealt with issues of all kinds, on and off the court. However, he has proven over his long basketball career that you always have an opportunity to make a difference for those around you. Even if you make mistakes one day, you can still work hard and make great decisions at the next opportunity.

Remember that Shaq's career - the four NBA championships, the three Finals MVPs, the league MVP, and the two league scoring championships - was all built on only a few years of hard work and practice. The man did not begin playing the sport at an organized level until the age of 16. That's remarkable!

He also played the game as fairly as possible. When he played against another player who was trying to draw fouls by exaggerating falls, O'Neal let the media know about his frustrations, saying, "I'm a guy with no talent who has gotten this way with hard work."

He did work hard to get to where he was. Looking back on his legacy, though, some are disappointed that he didn't achieve more on the court. Phil Jackson believed that Shaq could have been the MVP for 10 straight years if he had worked harder.

Regardless of Shaq's impact on the court, and on the game of basketball itself, one cannot deny that he is working hard to be the MVP of those in need around the country. He's taken everything he's been given and still found ways to give back, to make a difference.

Even when you have reached a point of comfort or success in your life, don't forget what it was like when you were struggling. Don't forget about those who helped, who gave you what they had, to give you a chance to move forward in your life. No man is an island, they say, and that includes one of the biggest men to ever play the game, Shaquille O'Neal.

CHAPTER 11:

BILL RUSSELL

Few professional athletes have attained as much success as Bill Russell, the first Black NBA player to reach the status of an NBA superstar. When discussing the best players to ever step onto the court, it would be a crime to keep Russell out of the conversation. However, as always, the path to the NBA was not an easy one for Russell, as he had to deal with a country and culture that was not very accepting of Black people.

Let's take a look at the life and legacy of Bill Russell, so we can see how greatness can rise above prejudice and hatred.

Bill was born in 1934 in West Monroe, Louisiana, a Southern US town that was heavily segregated, meaning that Black and White people lived in different areas, with Black people being relegated to the poorer areas. Russell remembered events when both of his parents had to deal with racism, so it was something that had a profound impact on his upbringing. Still, his family managed to avoid any major acts of violence.

When Russell was eight, his family moved west to Oakland, California, but they struggled and fell into poverty. When Bill was 12, his mother passed away unexpectedly. Bill had been especially close to her, so it was a difficult time for him. Bill watched how his father didn't give up and continued to work hard to provide for the family. The elder Russell's tenacity to provide imprinted on Bill, who would later call his father his hero.

As Bill entered middle school in Oakland, he had good athleticism, but the game of basketball did not come easily. At Herbert Hoover Junior High, Bill was cut from the school team during tryouts, as he simply did not have the skills of the game. It seemed like he would likely be a better fit for track and field, perhaps.

In high school, though, Bill's coach encouraged him to continue working on the game's fundamentals, as the coach had recognized his raw athletic talent. It was also a new experience because that coach, George Powles, was a White man. Bill's previous experiences with White men in positions of authority were not good ones, so to hear encouragement from a White man was a glimmer of hope for Bill.

It didn't take long for Bill to get a handle on how the game was played, and then change it completely for the better. When he was being taught how to play defense, coaches always instructed defenders to keep their feet flat on the ground, which would give them better reaction times to move left or right. However, Bill was not satisfied with this style of play. Instead, he began jumping with the offensive players to block shots or intercept passes.

His coaches tried to insist that he play the game as they knew how to coach it, but he ignored them - to his benefit.

Bill also found great value in memorizing his opponents' movements, looking for patterns and preparing for how to defend in those situations. He read as many sports magazines as he could to gather information on his opponents.

However, his fundamentals in the game were still lacking, so as his high school years came to a close, Bill was overlooked by almost every single college recruiter, except for one. Hal DeJulio of the University of San Francisco offered him a scholarship, which opened Bill's eyes to the possibility of basketball being his ticket out of racism and poverty. He accepted the offer immediately and vowed to make basketball his priority moving forward.

Thankfully, the coach at the university, Phil Woolpert, did not care about skin color when it came to his basketball team. Because he only cared about putting the best team on the floor, he became the first coach of a top-division college to start three Black players on the court, and Bill Russell was one of those three.

Russell's fundamentals still weren't great, but the defensive scheme that Coach Woolpert deployed was a fit for Russell's skills. Russell was not as big as some of the other centers he played against, so instead of trying to only guard the center, Russell would often use his speed, reach, and footwork to help defend against other shooters on the floor when he could cheat away from the center position.

Many basketball writers around the country quickly took notice, and *Sports Illustrated* even wrote of Russell that "If he ever learns to hit the basket, they're going to have to rewrite the rules."

And, of course, the NCAA did make a rule change based on Russell's tremendous defensive play, making the lane wider, meaning that he could not camp as close to the basket as before.

Aside from rule changes, Russell still had to deal with racism, particularly when traveling to areas of the country where those beliefs were still tolerated, or even celebrated.

But Bill Russell was not going to let racism interfere with his path moving forward. During his junior year, his team had a record of 28-1, and they captured the National Championship at the end of the year. Russell was named the MVP of the tournament, averaging more than 20 points and 20 rebounds per game. However, another player, a White player, was selected as the Northern California Player of the Year. It was in that moment that Russell decided to ignore individual accomplishments and focus on the success of his team.

He understood that racism and prejudice are stronger when attacking a single person. But, if they're going up against an entire team of people, their efforts are weaker.

As such, Russell and the University of San Francisco Dons would win another National Championship in 1956, and between the two years, the team had a winning streak of 55 games. Oh, and Russell also invented the alley-oop pass and dunk play with his teammate, K.C. Jones.

No big deal at this point, right? Bill Russell has only changed how basketball players play defense and invented one of the most spectacular plays in the game! And he did these things in the face of a country that did not want him to succeed. It's hard to get anything done when you know that everyone around you despises you.

Despite all of his success, racism still impacted Russell's path forward. The owner of the Harlem Globetrotters, Abe Saperstein had come calling to the University of San Francisco, seeking to sign Russell to his team. But Saperstein was only interested in discussing the offer with Russell's coach, not with Russell himself. Because of this insult, Russell refused the offer and decided to enter the NBA draft instead.

As the draft approached, it was clear that the Boston Celtics wanted to select him, but they were afraid that he would be picked by another team first. Phone calls were made, and there were even rumors that the Celtics owner had offered another team's owner tickets to the Ice Capades if they didn't draft Russell, but that cannot be fully verified.

Either way, the St. Louis Hawks drafted Russell with the second overall pick, then traded him to the Celtics for Ed Macauley, an all-star player who wanted to be in St. Louis. It was one of those trades where everyone got what they wanted, and now Bill Russell could begin his journey in the NBA.

But first, Russell was determined to represent his country in the 1956 Olympics. At this time, professionals could not play on the Olympic teams, so Russell would have to miss some of his rookie season to participate. That's exactly what he did, leading the US to a gold medal with eight straight wins. Over those eight games, the team's margin of victory was an average of 53.5 points!

With his entry into the NBA now prepared, Russell played 48 games in the 1956–57 season. He averaged just under 15 points per game but led the league with an average of 19.6 rebounds per contest.

In fact, his defense was so good, that the Celtics called their defensive scheme the "Hey, Bill" defense. Simply put, they would call for Bill to come and help them double-team an opponent because Bill was fast enough to interrupt another opponent and still get back in time to cover the man he left.

Even in the NBA, others were angry with Russell's success. He avoided interacting with fans from any team - even his own - because he was used to having to protect himself from people who wanted to cause him harm. The targeting of Russell happened even on the court until he decided to stand up for himself. Playing against the New York Knicks, their center, Ray Felix, harassed Russell throughout the game - until Russell knocked him out. Russell was fined $25, and no one ever harassed him on the court again.

In his first-ever playoff game, Russell recorded 16 points and a whopping 31 rebounds. The Celtics cruised to the NBA Finals, where they faced the St. Louis Hawks, the team that had drafted and traded Russell to the Celtics.

The 1957 Finals went the full seven games and featured a block from Russell that helped the Celtics reach overtime. The Hawks had one more chance to score and tie the game at the end of the second overtime, but it timed out, and the Celtics won their first NBA title.

The following season, Russell was voted the NBA Most Valuable Player, which is voted on by the players in the league. Media members vote for All-NBA teams, and their bias against him resulted in a second-team selection instead of a first-team. It was yet another example of the prejudice they had against him and the unique way he played the game.

The Celtics would have another successful year, but they would fall to the Hawks in the 1958 Finals after Russell missed two games with a foot injury. Many speculated that the Celtics would have won the series if Russell had been healthy, but that's how it goes in sports, sometimes.

Regardless, the Celtics knew what they had in Russell, and over the next eight years, the Celtics won the NBA Championship eight more times. That's right. In Russell's first 10 years in the NBA, he won *nine championships*.

Then, when Boston's coach retired, the search for a new coach began. After the first few players declined the position, Russell accepted the position, becoming the first Black NBA coach in the league's history. In his first season coaching the team (and also playing), they lost in the Eastern Division Finals to the heavily favored 76ers team.

After the series loss, Russell shared a special moment with his grandfather, whom Russell had brought back to the locker room for a tour after the game. Russell was showing his grandfather around when they passed the shower area. Russell's grandfather saw two Celtics players, one Black and one White, showering next to each other and discussing the game together.

Russell's grandfather began to cry. When Russell tried to figure out what was upsetting him, his grandfather told him that he was so proud of Bill, that he was leading a team consisting of men from different backgrounds, different ethnicities, and that these men could cooperate and get along with each other.

It was a moment that demonstrated to Russell just how far he had come through his NBA journey, and through American history, to reach the top of the NBA.

In the next two seasons, Russell led the Celtics to two more NBA Championships, one of which included the first-ever comeback from a 3-1 series deficit. After those championships, Bill Russell abruptly retired from basketball and also walked away from his coaching position.

Fans were upset, but Bill Russell had never felt as though he owed the fans anything, not after the way he had been treated by so many people across the country. Still, no one can argue against Bill Russell being the best defensive player of all time. Couple that with the era in which he did it, dealing with racism and prejudice wherever he went, it's a feat that will likely go unmatched.

In 2011, Bill Russell was honored by US President Barack Obama with the Presidential Medal of Freedom, which is the highest honor that can be awarded to an American civilian.

Bill Russell changed the game of basketball, and he did it against the wishes of almost everyone around him. He knew what was best for him, and for the game, and he did it. If you know what is best for you, or your ambitions, don't let naysayers try to keep you in line with them. Go chase your dream, and remember that hard work will be necessary to get you there.

CHAPTER 12:

KAREEM ABDUL-JABBAR

Activism can take many forms, and sometimes it comes in the form of domination on the basketball court. As the country around him was dealing with racism and prejudice in every aspect of society, Kareem Abdul-Jabbar found a path through the noise, using his basketball skills to set the stage for his argument against those that sought to push against Black Americans rising to prominence.

Let's examine the graceful game of Kareem Abdul-Jabbar, and the impact he made on the world around him as an activist against racism.

Kareem Abdul-Jabbar was born Ferdinand Alcindor Jr. in 1947. He grew up with his parents in Harlem, New York, and he often dealt with bullying from kids who made fun of how tall he was. By the time he was nine years old, he was already five feet, eight inches - and could slam dunk the basketball.

In high school, the bullying came to an end, especially when Ferdinand's high school team began winning. At Power Memorial Academy, he led his team on a 71-game winning streak over three seasons. He scored a record for New York City High School for points over that time, with 2,067 points. The nickname for Ferdinand that emerged from local media and the schools was "The Tower from Power."

However, during his senior year, Ferdinand's relationship with his coach soured after the coach called him a racial slur. The team would be runners-up for the New York City Catholic championship that season, but Ferdinand had other thoughts on his mind.

He wrote for a newspaper called the *Harlem Youth Action Project*, as he had become very interested in the Harlem riot of 1964, an event that started when a 15-year-old Black boy was shot by a New York police officer. Ferdinand became intrigued by the political side of this event. He knew it was something he would be working toward for quite a long time.

Although Ferdinand was already good enough to play in the NBA, the rules at that time only accepted players who were old enough to have completed a college program. He also could have gone to play with the Harlem Globetrotters, but he ultimately decided to play college basketball. Even college teams from areas of the country still practicing segregation were willing to bring him on. He was that good! Regardless, he opted for UCLA, the University of California, Los Angeles.

Ferdinand played on the freshman team his first year, as the rules also prevented him from playing varsity as a freshman. With three other All-Americans on his squad, their team dominated. In fact, when UCLA held their annual exhibition between the varsity and freshman teams,

Ferdinand and the freshman squad won, for the first time in school history.

For style, in his first game on the varsity squad during his sophomore season, Ferdinand scored 56 points, breaking the school record for most points in a single game. He broke that record in his first game. Just to clarify: he did not break the record for most points scored in a player's *first* game. It was the most points scored by a player in *any* UCLA game.

Throughout that sophomore season, Ferdinand averaged 29 points and led his team to a perfect record, 30 wins and zero losses, including the national championship. Of course, whenever a player sets fire to a league like Ferdinand Alcindor just did, there has to be a rule change to try and bring that player back down to everyone else's level. So, what was the ridiculous rule change they decided to go for?

They banned dunking!

They stopped letting college players dunk because Ferdinand Alcindor was too good.

Could you imagine the NBA banning the chase-down block because LeBron James was dominating the league? What if they took the three-point shot away because Steph Curry was winning too many titles?

Ridiculous. But this is the type of thing that Black players back then had to deal with. Everyone was working against them.

Of course, Ferdinand and UCLA found a way through. Throughout his three years on the varsity squad, the UCLA Bruins won 88 basketball games and lost only two, which meant that they also won three national championships. One of those losses came while Ferdinand was dealing with an eye injury, and the other came from the University of Southern California, who held onto the ball as much as possible since there was no shot clock forcing them to shoot the ball after 30 seconds.

Because of frequent eye injuries, Ferdinand Alcindor began wearing goggles to protect his eyes from the fingers of his opponents. Those goggles would soon be his hallmark in the NBA.

Over the summer before his senior year, Ferdinand Alcindor converted religions and adopted a new name, Kareem. When he was invited to try out for Team USA at the 1968 Summer Olympics, he declined and instead boycotted the Games, citing the USA's unequal treatment of Black people.

After graduating, Kareem left UCLA holding multiple records, all of which focused on scoring. He holds the first-, second-, and third-place records for most field goals in a season. He also had the highest scoring average, with the most free throw attempts, and the most points in a single game.

The Harlem Globetrotters offered Kareem $1 million to play for them, but he turned down the offer and chose to enter the NBA draft instead, where he was selected first overall by the Milwaukee Bucks. The Bucks, at this point in history, were only in their second season as a team. In fact, the first pick went to the Bucks after they won a coin toss with the Phoenix Suns. It's funny how history can be made with such small, insignificant moments that build up to significant ones.

The New York Nets of the American Basketball Association also drafted Kareem, and offered him more money in later rounds of offers, but he ultimately decided to play for the Bucks in the NBA.

After winning 27 games in their first season, Kareem helped the Bucks win 56 games in his rookie season, and he was voted the NBA Rookie of the Year. The following year, Kareem and Oscar Robertson led the Bucks to their first NBA championship. Kareem was named the Finals MVP, scoring 27 points per game on 60% shooting.

That following summer, Kareem, Robertson, and their coach went on a basketball tour in Africa. He requested that everyone start using his new name, Kareem Abdul-Jabbar instead of Ferdinand Alcindor. The following season, Abdul-Jabbar led the Bucks to the NBA Finals once more but lost to the Celtics in seven games. With Robertson retired, Abdul-Jabbar requested a trade but did not receive it. To make things worse, during the 1974–75 preseason, he suffered another eye scratch injury, and due to his frustration, he punched the backboard stanchion, breaking two bones in his hand. He ultimately missed 16 regular season games, and when he returned, the Bucks had a record of 3-13. He did his best to help the team after his return, but they finished in last place in their division, missing the playoffs.

During the offseason, Abdul-Jabbar finally secured his trade to the Los Angeles Lakers, but despite him winning the league MVP award, the Lakers missed the playoffs, and things were not looking any better for the next season. The Lakers had acquired no other well-known players to help Abdul-Jabbar, and most media pundits projected the Lakers to finish last in their division for the 1976–77 season.

However, to the surprise of all, Abdul-Jabbar put the team on his shoulders and the Lakers ended the season with the league's best record. Unfortunately, the Lakers were swept in the second round by the Trail Blazers.

Over the next two seasons, it was more of the same for Abdul-Jabbar and the Lakers, who could not reach the NBA Finals. But, with the arrival of Magic Johnson in 1979, things were looking up.

What followed over the next decade were eight trips to the Finals and five championships for the Lakers.

Kareem Abdul-Jabbar retired from the NBA at the end of the 1989 season, and when he did, he held the NBA records for most shots made and most minutes played. He had held the points record until LeBron James passed him in 2023.

In terms of his playing legacy, Abdul-Jabbar remains well known as an accurate shooter using a skyhook shot, which involves raising the ball in a hook motion, releasing it only when your hand reaches the apex of the hook. Because the ball is released so high, it is almost impossible to block.

During his basketball career, Abdul-Jabbar was also working hard as a writer and activist. He wrote and published an autobiography in 1983. He also wrote about the Harlem Renaissance, as well as Black army battalions during World War II. He has been outspoken about Islam and how it should not be blamed for extremists who choose to use violence.

It's one thing to try and help out those around you, but it's another thing entirely to take on a life of politics and criticism, as these arenas can often bring a lot of hatred and negative attention your way. Kareem Abdul-Jabbar was not going to be intimidated by anyone who sought to silence him, though. He was going to fight for the rights of minorities in the United States until everyone was treated equally.

Abdul-Jabbar was even appointed to positions in the US Government to further his advocacy. First, in 2012, Secretary of State Hillary Clinton appointed Abdul-Jabbar to a position as the cultural ambassador for the country. For this role, Abdul-Jabbar traveled to several countries around the world to help promote the education of children.

He was also appointed to the President's Council on Fitness, Sports, and Nutrition by President Barack Obama in 2016. He served in that office along with other professional athletes from the United States, including gymnast Gabrielle Douglas and soccer star Carli Lloyd.

Abdul-Jabbar made NBA history, but he also did his best to positively impact American history in the process. He wanted to help those who'd been persecuted by the government and society to get equal rights. His focus was always on getting it right. The NBA is a better organization for having him, as is the United States.

The next time you're allowed to fight for what is right, remember Kareem Abdul-Jabbar and his bravery in the face of racism and prejudice. Remember that making the right choice is better than going along with everyone else. It may not be easy, but you'll be much happier with the result.

CONCLUSION

The sport of basketball creates unique stars, as it is still one of the most accessible sports on the planet. That means that anyone from any background can make it to the highest heights of the game, and even end up representing their country on the international stage. Because of this accessibility, players often come from backgrounds that feature fewer opportunities and fewer resources than the more privileged.

It is an encouraging and inspiring thought that no matter where you are in life or your place in society, through hard work and practice, you can make a difference with a basketball. After all, each of the players in this story made an impact on a grand scale, shaking the very culture of this country.

Don't let the scale of their impacts discourage you. Any positive decision is good for you and the people around you. Think of it like a basketball bouncing in a puddle. It doesn't matter how big the ripples are. It only matters that the ripples are for positive results, not negative ones.

Kareem Abdul-Jabbar sought to fight against American racism culture, and Maya Moore used her platform to help reform criminal justice issues. Shaq wants to help kids in need, and Jimmy V just wanted to remind everyone to laugh, cry, and think. Magic Johnson helped the country learn more about HIV and AIDS, and the George Mason Patriots showed that anyone can rise and win in the biggest moment.

They all made impacts on those around them, and all of those impacts were of a different scale. Some of the individuals in this book simply changed how the game was played, or what could be expected of a basketball player. The possibilities are endless with a basketball in your hand.

Finally, remember that basketball is a sport that encourages your creativity. You don't have to play it exactly like everyone else does. You could use Abdul-Jabbar's skyhook, or you could focus on chase-down blocks like LeBron. Maybe your talents are on defense, like Bill Russell, or you want to shoot from anywhere on the court like Steph Curry. Even better, you could come up with something entirely new. The world of basketball can inspire you to find your own path.

Get dribbling!

Made in United States
Troutdale, OR
04/07/2024

18989644R00070